*To Alexandra, whose wisdom made me reconsider
my approach to many things.*

– R.C.J.

VIKING STUDIO

Published by the Penguin Group, Penguin Putnam Inc.,
375 Hudson Street, New York, New York 10014, U.S.A.
Penguin Books Ltd, 27 Wrights Lane, London W8 5TZ, England
Penguin Books Australia Ltd, Ringwood, Victoria, Australia
Penguin Books Canada Ltd, 10 Alcorn Avenue,
Toronto, Ontario, Canada M4V 3B2
Penguin Books (N.Z.) Ltd, 182-190 Wairau Road,
Auckland 10, New Zealand

Penguin Books Ltd, Registered Offices:
Harmondsworth, Middlesex, England

First American Edition published in 2000 by Viking Studio,
a member of Penguin Putnam Inc.

1 2 3 4 5 6 7 8 9 10

Copyright © R. C. Jamieson, 2000
Copyright © Frances Lincoln Ltd, 2000
Photographs of illustrations from Cambridge University Library Add.1464 and Add.1643
reproduced by permission of the Syndics of Cambridge University Library

ISBN 0-670-88934-2

CIP data available

Printed in China

Set in Baker Signet

Designed by Trish Going

The Perfection of Wisdom

Extracts from the *Aṣṭasāhasrikāprajñāpāramitā*

SELECTED AND TRANSLATED BY

R. C. JAMIESON

ILLUSTRATED WITH ANCIENT SANSKRIT MANUSCRIPTS

VIKING STUDIO

FOREWORD

For followers of the Mahāyāna or 'Great Vehicle' traditions of Buddhism, *The Perfection of Wisdom* sūtras represent the epitome of the Buddha's teachings. They contain advice not only on the wisdom understanding conventional and ultimate phenomena and on how to realize emptiness and dependent origination, but also on the fulfilment of the welfare of sentient beings. In other words, they deal with what we call wisdom and method, that is, the correct view of reality and the conduct or way of life of a bodhisattva, one who seeks enlightenment for the sake of all sentient beings.

When we distinguish between those scriptures that can be accepted as definitive and those that require interpretation, *The Perfection of Wisdom* is regarded as definitive. Customarily, when we arrange symbols to represent the Buddha's body, speech and mind, in addition to the statue or painting and stūpa that represent his body and mind, a scripture represents his speech. More often than not that scripture deals with the perfection of wisdom. Likewise, in ancient India and later in Tibet, it was considered an act of virtue to honour the practice of *The Perfection of Wisdom* by creating or sponsoring the creation of elaborate and illustrated editions.

However, that is not to say that these books are only to be admired from afar; they are also sources of great inspiration. I recall that before finally leaving my residence at the Norbulingka in Lhasa to escape to India, I sat down in my prayer room and read from one of *The Perfection of Wisdom* sūtras. I read until I reached a passage in which the Buddha told a disciple to be of good courage – only then did I get up to go.

This book on the perfection of wisdom will serve as an inspiration too. It not only attempts to convey some of the principal contents and spirit of the original scriptures in English that may be easily understood today, but also includes enchanting illustrations from the oldest Indian manuscript in existence. I am sure that readers will find it both illuminating and delightful.

H. H. THE DALAI LAMA

INTRODUCTION

Amongst the many Buddhist works in the collection at Cambridge University Library are two very important Sanskrit palm leaf manuscripts. Both about a thousand years old, they share one of the most famous titles in world literature – *Aṣṭasāhasrikāprajñāpāramitā* or *The Perfection of Wisdom in 8,000 Lines*. One of these manuscripts is thought to be the oldest dated illustrated Indian manuscript in the world, and the other is dated just a few years later. For the first time, this book reproduces in colour all the illustrations from the oldest manuscript, and many of the illustrations from the other.

The Perfection of Wisdom is a new translation of extracts from *The Perfection of Wisdom in 8,000 Lines*. Composed in south India between 100 BCE and 100 CE, this is the earliest in a long tradition of various *Perfection of Wisdom* texts. In the course of its history, the basic *Perfection of Wisdom* has been expanded to 18,000, 25,000 and 100,000 lines, and shortened to 300 lines (*The Diamond Sūtra*) and 25 or 14 lines (*The Heart Sūtra*). This development went so far as to create *The Perfection of Wisdom in One Letter*, which consists simply of the letter 'A' (in Buddhism 'A' has a special affinity with voidness).

In this translation, the aim is to express clearly and accurately the meaning of the original text in words that the modern English speaker understands, while retaining the integrity of the original. So, for example, the speakers employ many more forms of polite address than would be natural today because, at the time of writing, it would have been impolite not to use these terms. Indra, the famous chief of the gods, is often called Śakra, and is addressed as Kauśika. Epithets such as Sugata (Well-Gone) or Tathāgata (Thus-Gone) are used to refer to the Buddha. The text is also inclined towards lists and repetition, which served as emphasis in an oral tradition where memorizing was important.

At first sight, *The Perfection of Wisdom* is bewildering, full of paradox and apparent irrationality. Yet once one accepts that trying to unravel these texts without experiencing the intuitions behind them is not satisfactory, it becomes clear that paradox and irrationality are the only means of conveying to the reader those underlying intuitions that would otherwise be impossible to express. Edward Conze succinctly summarized what *The Perfection of Wisdom* is about, saying, 'The thousands of lines of the *Prajñāpāramitā* can be summed up in the following two sentences: 1) One should become a bodhisattva (or, Buddha-to-be), i.e. one who is content with nothing less than all-knowledge attained through the perfection of wisdom for the sake of all beings. 2) There is no such thing as a bodhisattva, or as all-knowledge, or as a 'being', or as the perfection of wisdom, or as an attainment. To accept both of these contradictory facts is to be perfect.'[1]

The central idea of *The Perfection of Wisdom* is complete release from the world of existence. *The Perfection of Wisdom* goes beyond earlier Buddhist teaching that focused on the rise and fall of phenomena to state that there can be no such rise and fall – because all phenomena are essentially void. The earlier perception had been that reality is composed of a multiplicity of things. *The Perfection of Wisdom* states that there is no multiplicity: all is one. Even existence (saṃsāra) and nirvāṇa are essentially the same, and both are ultimately void. The view of *The Perfection of Wisdom* is that words and analysis have a practical application in that they are necessary for us to function in this world but, ultimately, nothing can be predicated about anything.

Within this context of voidness, *The Perfection of Wisdom* offers a way to enlightenment. It represents the formal introduction to Buddhist thought of a practical ideal – the ideal of a bodhisattva. Unlike an arhat or pratyekabuddha, beings who achieve enlightenment but cannot pass on the means of enlightenment to others, a bodhisattva should and does teach. A bodhisattva must practise the six perfections: giving, morality, patience, vigour, contemplation and wisdom. Wisdom is the most important of these because it dispels the darkness of sensory delusion and allows things to be seen as they really are.

The Perfection of Wisdom is set in the community of monks at the Vulture Peak, Rājagṛha (Rajgir

[1] Edward Conze, *The Prajñāpāramitā Literature* (1960), p. 15.

in modern Bihar) – a place which can be visited to this day. The text takes the form of a conversation-circle where who is speaking can be as important as what is said. Śāriputra represents the outlook of traditional Buddhist teaching, presented as a valuable but inferior kind of knowledge. The other disciples, Subhūti and Pūrṇa, understand the doctrine much more thoroughly than Śāriputra – especially Subhūti, who often represents just what the Buddha himself would say. Ānanda, the Buddha's first cousin and foremost disciple, is frequently addressed by the Buddha. Since he heard all of the Buddha's teachings, he speaks to authenticate the Buddha's words. The Buddhas who appear in these extracts are the historical Buddha and the future Buddha, Maitreya, who here is a very advanced bodhisattva. Maitreya's role is to expound the most difficult philosophical points.

THE ILLUSTRATIONS

The two manuscripts featured in this book are Add.1464[2] and Add.1643[3], both kept in Cambridge University Library. The first is the oldest dated illustrated Sanskrit manuscript in the world (997 CE)[4], while the second is the oldest dated illustrated Nepalese manuscript in the world (1015 CE). Both manuscripts were produced during the reign of Mahīpāla I, the Pāla king who, between 992–1042 CE, ruled over what are now parts of northern India and Nepal.

Given that the nature of the medium, the palm leaf, places many restrictions on what an artist can do, the variety and detail in the illustratations of these manuscripts is astonishing. The primary purpose of the paintings was to protect the manuscripts and serve as objects of meditation, and they do not relate closely to the text. The stūpa, which represents the Buddha and his final entry into nirvāṇa, is a common symbol. Trees such as the pipal tree, under which the Buddha was enlightened, and the sal tree, under which he was born, also appear often. The throne is an important theme, as is the wheel, which represents the turning of the wheel of Buddhist teaching. A Buddha is represented much like a god or king rather than as a simple ascetic. Long ears reflect the weight of heavy jewelled earrings, and his hair is in the pronounced

---

[2] 227 folios, 5 x 53.5 cm, talipot leaves, 15 illustrations of 5 x 4.5 cm.

[3] 223 folios, 5.25 x 54 cm, talipot leaves, 85 illustrations (88 originally, 3 lost from the replaced first leaf, a paper replacement) of 5.25 x 6 cm.

[4] Dated in the fifth year of Mahīpāla, a year corresponding with A.D. 997 or possibly a few years earlier, depending on the exact date of Mahīpāla's accession.

top-knot of a king without his turban. However, he does not wear fancy clothes or jewels and his attire is that of a religious figure, usually clinging closely to his body and often leaving the right arm free. Certain events from the Buddha's life feature prominently: his birth in the Lumbinī grove, Māra's attack at Bodhgayā, his first teaching in the Deer Park at Sārnāth, his death at Kuśinagara. The Buddha multiplying his forms at Śrāvasti, the attack by an elephant at Rājagṛha, the monkeys giving him honey at Vaiśali, and his return to Sāṃkāśya after teaching his mother in heaven are also highlighted.

An impressive variety of sites in these paintings, displaying a fascinating diversity of architecture and dress, reflects the spread of Buddhism over Asia and a tradition of pilgrimage. The kingdom of Mahīpāla I included many important Buddhist shrines, so pilgrims from other countries would have been frequent visitors. The illustrations feature specific temples in China, Java, Śrī Laṅkā, Gujarat, Konkan, Pakistan and Bangladesh, as well as the more local shrines in eastern India. It is unlikely that the painter had travelled to all these places; he probably gained his information from other manuscript illustrations or from large paintings on cloth or walls.[5]

The patron of the oldest manuscript is named as Lāḍakā, the daughter of Bahubhūti (who would have been a wealthy Indian). It was the practice for donors to sponsor monks to copy and illuminate sacred texts in return for the spiritual benefit to themselves and their families. The manuscripts themselves did not pass into the donor's possession, but remained with the monastery. We do not know where Lāḍakā's manuscript was copied, but the other manuscript was first copied in 1015 CE at Śrī Hlam monastery in Nepal. In 1139 CE, a colophon was added to this later manuscript which says that *The Perfection of Wisdom* was rescued 'when fallen into the hands of unbelievers'. By 1200 CE these 'unbelievers' had the upper hand in eastern India and – since few, if any, individuals would have had private collections of manuscripts – the resulting destruction of Buddhist monasteries, libraries and universities had a disastrous effect on the survival of India's manuscript heritage. The great era of manuscript production came to an end and most of the earliest surviving Indian manuscripts have been found, like the two featured here, in the temple libraries of Nepal, or in other places in central Asia.[6]

[5] For more information about the illustrations, see pp.104-106.

[6] The reader who would like to take a greater interest in this material can turn to the original Sanskrit, in a scholarly edition of Rājendralāla Mitra's *Ashtasāhasrikā* and to a complete translation of the text, in Edward Conze's *The Perfection of Wisdom in Eight Thousand Lines*. The manuscripts can be ordered on microfilm or CD-ROM from the Photography Department of Cambridge University Library. Much more than this brief glimpse of *The Perfection of Wisdom* can be achieved, both through further reading and in scholarship that still needs to be done. rcj10@cam.ac.uk.

Subhūti's Task

The Lord Buddha said to the venerable
Subhūti the Elder, "Make it clear, Subhūti, to
the bodhisattvas, the great beings, beginning
with the perfection of wisdom, how
bodhisattvas, great beings, go forth into the
perfection of wisdom." [3]

A bodhisattva's development commences with his production of the thought of enlightenment. The thought of enlightenment is a mental attitude: the aspiration to become an enlightened being, a Buddha, which starts with the desire to become a bodhisattva. This thought marks the beginning of a bodhisattva's long journey towards Buddhahood.

As Subhūti, one of the foremost exponents of the Buddha's teachings, explains to Śāriputra, a disciple with less understanding, *The Perfection of Wisdom* goes one step beyond this widely accepted concept to question the existence of thought in general and even the existence of that most important thought, the thought of enlightenment.

THE THOUGHT OF ENLIGHTENMENT

"Moreover, Lord Buddha, when a bodhisattva, a great being, practises the perfection of wisdom and develops the perfection of wisdom, the bodhisattva does not take pride in what he has learnt. The reason for that is that the original source of the thought, that a thought is no thought, is obvious."

Śāriputra asked, "Venerable Subhūti, does that thought which is no thought exist?"

Subhūti replied, "Venerable Śāriputra, is this which is no thought a no thought which exists or does not exist? Is it known or perceived?"

Śāriputra said, "Venerable Subhūti, it is not."

Subhūti said, "Venerable Śāriputra, if this no thought exists or does not exist or is not known or is not perceived, then is it even a sensible question when you asked if that thought which is no thought exists?" [5-6]

The Perfection of Wisdom provides early definitions, from various standpoints, of a bodhisattva. As a being (sattva) whose purpose is enlightenment (bodhi) for himself and others, and as a great being (mahāsattva), a bodhisattva is central to the perfection of wisdom.

Śāriputra and Subhūti's discussion of the term 'great being' shows how a bodhisattva is detached from 'adverse influences' (āsrava) – the ties such as passion, desire for existence, wrong views, and ignorance, which bind a person to rebirth.

Pūrṇa, a disciple who travelled and taught in hazardous areas, employs strong military imagery in his interpretation of a great being. The greatness of the mahāsattva is derived from the great armour of the Mahāyāna itself, the Great Vehicle. Pūrṇa's words serve to encourage those exposed to difficulties in the course of their teaching, as he himself faced considerable physical danger in his travels. A bodhisattva is never timid.

THE MEANING OF THE TERM 'BODHISATTVA'

"Subhūti, a 'bodhi-sattva' (enlightenment-being), a great being, is called that because his purpose is enlightenment." [18]

THE MEANING OF THE TERM 'GREAT BEING'

"A bodhisattva, a 'great being' (mahā-sattva), is called that because his purpose is greatness, greatness for multitudes of beings, he devotes himself to the mass of beings." [18]

Śāriputra and Subhūti Discuss the Term 'Great Being'

The venerable Śāriputra said, "A bodhisattva is called a 'great being' because he demonstrates teachings to repudiate various wrong views, such as speculations about the self, about sentient beings, about life, about the soul, about existence, about annihilation, about destruction, about eternity, about individuality, and the like."

Then the venerable Subhūti said to the Lord Buddha, "It is perfectly clear to me, Lord Buddha, why a bodhisattva is called a 'great being'."

The Lord Buddha replied, "Then, Subhūti, make it perfectly clear what you are thinking now."

Subhūti said, "Lord Buddha, a bodhisattva is called a 'great being' because the thought of enlightenment, the thought of all-embracing knowledge, thought without adverse influences, unequalled thought, thought beyond that of all the disciples and pratyekabuddhas, these are not subject to or involved in thought.

"Why? Because though the thought of all-embracing knowledge does not involve adverse influences, even this thought of all-embracing knowledge, which does not involve adverse influences, is not subject to or involved in thought. This is the reason a bodhisattva is summed up as a great being."

Then the venerable Śāriputra asked the venerable Subhūti, "How, venerable Subhūti, can it not be subject to or involved in thought?"

Subhūti replied, "It is not subject to or involved in thought because there is no thought." [19]

PŪRṆA'S VIEW OF THE TERM 'GREAT BEING'

Pūrṇa, son of Maitrāyānī, said to the Lord Buddha, "A great being, Lord Buddha, is called 'great being' (mahā-sattva). Armed with great armour, that being sets out on the great vehicle (mahā-yāna), and mounted upon the great vehicle, that great being goes by the name 'mahā-sattva'." [20]

The following paradoxical statement, that a bodhisattva leads others to nirvāṇa, while not leading anyone to nirvāṇa, illustrates one of the key themes of *The Perfection of Wisdom*, the essentially illusory nature of everything that is perceived. From worldly phenomena to nirvāṇa itself, all things are as illusory as a magician's trick – including the teaching, the 'nothing at all' that Subhūti expounds to the gods. Understanding this is a part of the process of enlightenment, and by teaching others that even nirvāṇa is an illusion, a bodhisattva helps them realize it. Wherever a bodhisattva might teach, he is protected by this 'great armour', since there is nothing to fear when perceived dangers may prove to be simply illusory.

The gods' longing for success in the various stages of practice, as a novice, as a once-returner, as an arhat exempt from further rebirths, or in enlightenment itself, implies recognition of the self and the existence of something called nirvāṇa. Longing for that success prevents it. A bodhisattva does not desire nirvāṇa for himself, but chooses to remain in this world for the sake of others.

A MAGICIAN'S ILLUSION

The Lord Buddha said, "Subhūti, here a bodhisattva, a great being, thinks, 'I should lead countless beings to nirvāṇa. I should lead innumerable beings to nirvāṇa. But no-one exists who can be led to nirvāṇa by anyone.' And still, he leads those sentient beings to nirvāṇa. Yet there is no being who is led to nirvāṇa, nor is anybody led to nirvāṇa by anyone.

"Why? Subhūti, the inherent nature of phenomena should be assumed to be inherently illusory. Subhūti, a talented magician, or even a magician's apprentice, might conjure up a great crowd of people at a crossroads, and then make that great crowd of people

that has been conjured up, disappear. Subhūti, what do you think about that? Was anyone there really created or killed or destroyed or made to disappear?"

Subhūti replied, "No, Lord Buddha."

The Lord Buddha said, "Similarly, Subhūti, a bodhisattva, a great being, leads countless, innumerable beings to nirvāṇa. And yet there is no being who is led to nirvāṇa, nor is anybody led to nirvāṇa by anyone. After hearing the idea set out in this explanation, a bodhisattva, a great being, is then neither frightened, nor terrified, nor overcome with trembling. To that extent, Subhūti, a bodhisattva, a great being, can be known as armed with great armour." [20-21]

THE LIMITS OF ANALYSIS

"Then, venerable Subhūti, is production a phenomenon which is not produced? Is non-production a phenomenon which is produced?"

He replied, "Venerable Śāriputra, talking about 'a produced phenomenon which is a non-produced phenomenon' clearly makes no sense." [30]

Subhūti Teaches Nothing?

Some of the gods present there in that assembly thought, "We understand the prattling yakṣas, the yakṣas' speech, the yakṣas' bellowing, the yakṣas' sentences, the yakṣas' discussions, the yakṣas' mumbling. But we do not understand what Subhūti the Elder mumbles, teaches and explains!"

The venerable Subhūti, with the authority of the Buddha, after noticing how they were thinking, discussed the reasoning of these gods, "The gods do not know or understand this. So, nothing at all is being communicated here, nothing at all is being learned."

Then the gods thought, "Please expand on this, noble Subhūti! Please expand on this, noble Subhūti! The noble Subhūti devotes himself to the remoter than remote. The noble Subhūti devotes himself to, shows and explains the subtler than subtle, the deeper than deep."

The venerable Subhūti, with the authority of the Buddha, after noticing how they were thinking, discussed the reasoning of these gods, "Therefore, gods, one who longs for the success of a novice, longing for the success of a novice, never reaches the peace of a non-returner. One who longs for the success of a once-returner, longing for the success of a once-returner, or who longs for the success of an arhat, longing to be an arhat, or who longs for the success of personal enlightenment, longing for personal enlightenment, never reaches the peace of a non-returner.

One who longs for the success of the highest complete enlightenment, longing for the highest complete enlightenment, never reaches the peace of a non-returner." [38-39]

Perfection of wisdom is not found in the five components of personal existence (the five skandha: form, feeling, perception, mental activities and consciousness) which constitute what we mistake to be the self. However it is also not realized through anything else, through the opposite or the negative of these things.

One should not try to grasp the perfection of wisdom in these terms, but instead look for it in Subhūti's teachings. When Subhūti speaks, he does so with the authority of the Tathāgata, the Lord Buddha. Much of the teaching in *The Perfection of Wisdom* is put forward through similes, paradoxes and dialogue, which are used to point out illusion, rather than through a direct approach.

Śakra, king of the gods, is the god Indra. He is addressed as Kauśika.

WHERE TO FIND PERFECT WISDOM

Śakra, king of the gods, asked the venerable Śāriputra, "Where, noble Śāriputra, should a bodhisattva, a great being, seek the perfection of wisdom?"

Śāriputra replied, "Kauśika, a bodhisattva, a great being, should seek the perfection of wisdom in the venerable Subhūti's discussions."

Śakra, king of the gods, asked the venerable Śāriputra, "Noble Śāriputra, this perfection of wisdom, of which the noble Subhūti speaks, is based on whose opinion, on whose authority is it known?"

The venerable Śāriputra replied, "Kauśika, this perfection of wisdom, of which the noble Subhūti speaks, is based on the opinion of the Tathāgata, is known on the authority of the Tathāgata."

Then the venerable Subhūti said to Śakra, king of the gods, "Kauśika, you ask on whose opinion is based this perfection of wisdom, of which the noble Subhūti speaks, on whose authority is it known? Kauśika, this perfection of wisdom of which I speak is based on the opinion of the Tathāgata, is known on the authority of the Tathāgata.

"Similarly, Kauśika, you ask where a bodhisattva, a great being, should seek the perfection of wisdom? Kauśika, a bodhisattva, a great being, does not seek the perfection of wisdom in form or in that which is not form. Neither does he seek it in feeling, nor in perception, nor in mental activities, nor in consciousness. Why? Because the perfection of wisdom is neither form nor other than form. The perfection of wisdom is neither feeling, perception, mental activities, consciousness, nor other than them." [43-44]

Reverence of relics brings merit, but much more is to be gained from the devotion to and spreading of the perfection of wisdom. Anyone who reveres all-embracing knowledge will find they can revere the perfection of wisdom.

In Buddhism, all-embracing knowledge (sarvajñajñāna) does not necessarily mean omniscience, in the sense of knowing and seeing all things at once. However, a Buddha's knowledge is equal to that of any other teacher claiming omniscience, since he teaches only about what is relevant and does not engage in inappropriate questions. A Buddha employs terms which are intelligible to his listeners. He does not speak to people about concepts which they will not comprehend, just as when he speaks to gods, he does not use ideas that are not applicable to them.

REVERENCE FOR ALL-EMBRACING KNOWLEDGE

"After I have gone to parinirvāṇa my relics will be revered. In that regard, Kauśika, any worthy son or worthy daughter will, having written or copied this perfection of wisdom, become devoted to it, and will honour, adore, respect, revere, pay homage to and esteem it, with divine flowers, incense, perfumes, garlands, oils, powders, robes, parasols, banners, bells and flags.

"Kauśika, this will bring more merit to that worthy son or daughter. Why? Kauśika, the worthy son or daughter who will revere all-embracing knowledge, that worthy son or daughter honours, adores, respects, reveres, pays homage to and esteems the writing or copying of the perfection of wisdom, and they will perform various acts of reverence to it and from this gain greater merit. Why? Because, Kauśika, anyone who reveres all-embracing knowledge will revere the perfection of wisdom." [58-59]

The Buddha often peppered his teachings with similes, lively images drawing upon a full range of human experiences, in order to illustrate and clarify some of his more difficult philosophical points. The breadth and variety of similes is impressive: the change of seasons; sun, moon, and stars; lakes, rivers, oceans, and ships; jewels, food, trees, and flowers; lions, elephants, dogs, cows, hawks, and crows; arts and crafts; love, courtship, motherhood, and warfare; monarchs, cooks, accountants, merchants, goldsmiths, and outcasts – all these themes, and many more, serve to amplify the message of the teachings: the message of a clear and practical way to the extinction of suffering, the central point of Buddhist teaching.

THE SIMILE OF THE PEARLS

"All-embracing knowledge is in the perfection of wisdom. It is much like, Lord Buddha, among all the great jewels, those jewels that come from the ocean are sought in the ocean. Similarly, Lord Buddha, one should seek the great jewel of all-embracing knowledge in the ocean of the perfection of wisdom of the supreme, truly perfectly enlightened arhats, the Tathāgatas."

The Lord Buddha said to Śakra, king of the gods, "This is so, Kauśika, this is so. The great jewel, the all-embracing knowledge of the supreme, truly perfectly enlightened arhats, the Tathāgatas, comes forth from the ocean of the perfection of wisdom." [80]

There are six perfections – the perfection of giving (dāna), morality (śīla) patience (kṣānti), vigour (vīrya), contemplation (dhyāna), and wisdom (prajñā). The first five perfections describe a bodhisattva's practical approach to life but, as the Buddha explains to Ānanda (his personal attendant), these five are encompassed in the sixth perfection, the perfection of wisdom, without which they could well be ineffective.

Roots of virtue (kuśalamūla) are spiritual roots planted to aid in spiritual progress. Three roots of virtue are often cited in Buddhist literature – the avoidance of greed, the avoidance of malice and the avoidance of delusions. These, if developed intelligently, will over time help a bodhisattva gather a stock of good merit and aid him in his progress towards enlightenment.

While wisdom is the insight, skill in means (upaya-kauśalya) is the strategic thinking of a bodhisattva's advancement. These means may only be provisional, the different methods which a bodhisattva employs at various stages of his development. Since each method might eventually be abandoned, a bodhisattva takes care not to become too attached to any individual practice for its own sake.

THE FIRST FIVE PERFECTIONS

The venerable Ānanda said to the Lord Buddha, "The Lord Buddha does not describe the perfection of giving, he does not cite it by name. The Lord Buddha does not describe or cite by name the perfection of morality, the perfection of patience, the perfection of vigour or the perfection of contemplation. The Lord Buddha only describes and cites by name the perfection of wisdom."

The Lord Buddha replied, "This is so, Ānanda, this is so. I describe and cite by name the perfection of wisdom and not the other perfections. Why? Ānanda, the five previous perfections are constituent parts of the perfection of wisdom. What do you think

about that, Ānanda? Would giving, not developed in all-embracing
knowledge, be called the perfection of giving?

The venerable Ānanda replied, "No, Lord Buddha."

The Lord Buddha asked, "What do you think about that Ānanda?
Do you think that undeveloped morality, undeveloped patience,

undeveloped vigour, undeveloped contemplation, that wisdom, not developed in all-embracing knowledge, would be called the perfection of wisdom?"

Ānanda replied, "No, Lord Buddha."

The Lord Buddha asked, "Do you think, Ānanda, that the wisdom which develops the roots of virtue by developing all-embracing knowledge is inconceivable?"

Ānanda replied, "Yes, Lord Buddha, yes it is, Sugata. Wisdom, Lord Buddha, which develops the roots of virtue by developing all-embracing knowledge is inconceivable; that wisdom, Lord Buddha, is perfectly inconceivable."

The Lord Buddha said, "Therefore, Ānanda, the perfection of wisdom derives its name from its perfectedness, by which the roots of virtue developed in all-embracing knowledge take the name perfection. Therefore, Ānanda, the perfection of wisdom, through the roots of virtue developed in all-embracing knowledge, takes in and encompasses the five other constituent perfections. By this joining together the remaining five perfections are within the perfection of wisdom. Ānanda, this perfection of wisdom is just a synonym for the wholly accomplished six perfections. Therefore, Ānanda, in citing the perfection of wisdom, all six perfections are cited. Ānanda, just as seeds scattered in the earth grow to complete maturity, and the earth is the ground for these seeds, and the seeds grow dependent upon the earth, similarly, Ānanda, the five perfections which come under the perfection of wisdom are grounded in all-embracing knowledge. The five perfections grow, dependent upon the perfection of wisdom. Enveloped in the perfection of wisdom, they are called 'perfections'. Therefore, Ānanda, the perfection of wisdom on its own takes in and encompasses the five previous constituent perfections." [80-82]

THE SIMILE OF THE FABULOUS JEWEL

"Lord Buddha, it [the perfection of wisdom] is like a priceless, fabulous jewel with the physical quality of preventing the entrance of humans or ghosts wherever it has been placed. If a ghost haunted any man or woman, they could be rid of that ghost simply by laying out this fabulous jewel. Placing that fabulous jewel against a body distressed in its breathing of air would moderate, control, and calm that flow of air. Placing that fabulous jewel against a body fevered by bile would moderate, control, and calm that bile. Placing that fabulous jewel against a body completely distressed when overcome by phlegm would moderate, control, and calm that phlegm. Placing it against a body suffering from a disease with complications would moderate, control, and calm that disease ..."

... the venerable Ānanda asked Śakra, king of the gods, "Do these fabulous jewels exist only in the world of the gods, or do these fabulous jewels also belong to people here in India?"

Śakra replied, "Noble Ānanda, these fabulous jewels are with the gods. In comparison the fabulous jewels of people here in India seem coarse, trifling, rudimentary, lacking calibre, and so not displaying much physical quality. They do not approach a hundredth part of those divine jewels. They do not approach a thousandth, a hundred thousandth, a ten millionth, a billionth, a ten billionth, a trillionth, a quintillionth part of them! They are incomparable, they do not approach comparison in any fraction, a million, a billion, or a trillion. But those among the gods are exquisite, in all aspects abounding with qualities. If such a fabulous jewel were flung or tossed into a basket, and that fabulous jewel were then taken out of the basket, even the basket alone would be desirable. Desire would arise there simply from the qualities of the fabulous jewel cast aside from the basket.

"Similarly, Lord Buddha, these relics of a truly perfectly enlightened arhat, a Tathāgata gone to parinirvāṇa, are honoured because of the qualities of all-embracing knowledge from the perfection of wisdom. These relics of the Tathāgata are the repositories of all-embracing knowledge. Lord Buddha, just as instruction in the teachings of the Lord Buddhas in all worlds should be honoured, because it was acquired from the perfection of wisdom, so instruction in the teachings of any teacher of these teachings should be honoured, because it was acquired from the perfection of wisdom. Lord Buddha, just as the person of a king should be honoured, because his royal authority gives security to a body of people, so a teacher of these teachings should be honoured, because his authority in the body of the teachings (dharmakāya) gives security to a body of people. The teaching of these teachings and any teacher of these teachings is honoured, just as the Tathāgata's relics are honoured." [96-99]

40

Śakra's Naive Question

Śakra, king of the gods, asked the Lord Buddha, "Does a bodhisattva, a great being, practise only the perfection of wisdom and not the other perfections?"

The Lord Buddha replied, "Kauśika, a bodhisattva, a great being, practises all six perfections. But it is the perfection of wisdom that is central to a bodhisattva when he gives a gift, or guards morality, or exercises patience, or exerts vigour, or enters into contemplation, or finds insight into things. No difference or distinction is perceived between these six perfections, upheld by skill in means, developing the perfection of wisdom, developing all-embracing knowledge, just as no difference or distinction is conceived between the shadows cast by different trees in India. Their colours and shapes, their leaves, flowers and fruits, their height and circumference may vary, yet they are all simply called 'shadows'. Similarly, no difference or distinction is perceived between these six perfections, upheld by skill in means, developing the perfection of wisdom, developing all-embracing knowledge." [100-101]

THE SIMILE OF BLINDNESS

"Kauśika, it is not easy for people born blind to go to a village, town or settlement, because without a guide they cannot easily follow the path, be they a hundred, or a thousand, or a hundred thousand strong. Similarly, Kauśika, giving, morality, patience, vigour and contemplation can be outside the perfection of wisdom, and to be without the perfection of wisdom is like being born blind. How can one ever reach all-embracing knowledge, being without a guide to follow the path to all-embracing knowledge? When, Kauśika, giving, morality, patience, vigour and contemplation are encompassed by the perfection of wisdom, then they are termed 'perfection' rather than perfections. For then these five perfections follow the path to all-embracing knowledge, reaching all-embracing knowledge. It is like regaining sight!" [172-173]

ष्ठाच
माप
एकाष
काषि
ख्मय

Our inclination is to analyze, to place things in philosophical categories, but in absolute terms these categories are meaningless. They include what are described as the components of personal existence, the elements and the bases of sense perception. The components of personal existence are the five skandha: form, feeling, perception, mental activities and consciousness, which together constitute what is mistaken to be the self. The elements (dhātu) are what make up the material world: earth, water, fire, air and so on. The bases of sense perception (āyatana) constitute the senses: sight, hearing, smell, taste, touch and mind.

Each of these senses and sense objects can be described as distinct since, although they interact, the apparent coherence of anything is, in absolute terms, no more than an illusion. The senses and sense objects are tranquil in that they can only be perceived when both observer and observed are calm. One should meditate on an object as it really is, quiescent and isolated from the confusion of events, where emotions and the impact of other senses prevent concentration.

Ultimately, rather than analyzing the world as dual or as undivided, rather than further categorization, it is the practice of the perfection of wisdom that is recommended.

THE PERFECTION OF WISDOM

Then Subhūti said to the venerable Lord Buddha, "But it is possible to hear the perfection of wisdom, to distinguish, to concentrate on, to grasp, or to comprehend it. It is possible to explain or to listen to this perfection of wisdom by its appearance, characteristics and distinctive features, and to say that this is the perfection of wisdom here, or that that is the perfection of wisdom there?"

The Lord Buddha replied, "Subhūti, no, it's not. No, it's not Subhūti. It is not possible, Subhūti, to explain, to hear, to distinguish, to concentrate on, to grasp, or to comprehend this perfection of wisdom in terms of the components of personal existence, in terms of the elements, or in terms of the bases of sense perception. Why? Because, Subhūti, of the distinctness of all

phenomena, the total distinctness of all phenomena. But, Subhūti, it is not possible either to explain, to hear, to distinguish, to concentrate on, to grasp or to comprehend the perfection of wisdom through anything other than the components of personal existence, the elements, or the bases of sense perception.

"Yet bear the perfection of wisdom in mind. Why? Because, Subhūti, the components of personal existence, the elements, or the bases of sense perception are void, distinct and tranquil. The perfection of wisdom and the components of personal existence, the elements, or the bases of sense perception are not dual, are not divided. Because of their voidness and indivisibility and because of their tranquillity, they are not perceived. That which is not perceived about all phenomena, that is called the perfection of wisdom. Where there is no consciousness, no names, no words, no designations, that is called the perfection of wisdom." [177]

THE SIMILE OF LEAVING THE FOREST

"Lord Buddha, a man might come out of a forested wilderness one hundred, two hundred, three hundred, four hundred, five hundred, or even a thousand miles wide, and he might detect certain clues that indicate in advance signs of a village, a town, or a settlement. Clues such as a cowherd, a herdsman, a landmark, a nicely turned out garden, a well-managed wood, or other signs; clues seen that afterwards would turn out to be correct. He would think, 'Detecting these clues, I must be near a village, a town, or a settlement.' He relaxes; not worrying about thieves any more. Similarly, Lord Buddha, it should be understood that a bodhisattva, a great being, approaching this deep perfection of wisdom, would realize, 'I am near supreme, truly perfect enlightenment; supreme, truly perfect enlightenment is imminent.' Then, being at the stage of a disciple or the stage of a pratyekabuddha would not be alarming, would not be terrifying, and would not be feared. Why? Because he sees these advance clues to hold true for him, which is to say, he realizes the depth of the perfection of wisdom, to see, to praise, to honour, and to hear." [215-216]

THE SIMILE OF THE OCEAN

The venerable Śāriputra said to the Lord Buddha, "A man, Lord Buddha, who would like to see the ocean, might set out to see the ocean. As he sets out to see the ocean, if he should see bushes or any sign of bushes, or mountains or any sign of mountains ahead, he would know that at that point the ocean is still far off. If he no longer sees bushes or any sign of bushes, or mountains or any sign of mountains ahead, he would know that the ocean might at that point be near. Why? Because of the clue that the ocean, on which there are no bushes or any sign of bushes, or mountains or any sign of mountains, gradually slopes away to the horizon. Though he may not yet see the ocean clearly with his own eyes, nevertheless he comes to the conclusion, 'I am near the ocean, from here I am no longer a long way off from the ocean.' Similarly, Lord Buddha, a bodhisattva, a great being, should understand this deep perfection of wisdom, 'Though I may not have had a face to face prediction from the supreme, truly perfectly enlightened arhats, the Tathāgatas, yet I am near the manifestation of supreme, truly perfect enlightenment.' Why? Because he realizes the depth of the perfection of wisdom, to see, to praise, to honour, and to hear." [216-217]

The welfare of others is much more relevant to the perfection of wisdom than self-examination. The perfection of wisdom cannot be apprehended through the senses, it cannot be revealed by analysis of the components of the illusory self. This is why a bodhisattva teaches, helping others towards enlightenment. A bodhisattva's compassion is practised and developed primarily by giving. Giving the teachings, explaining the inconceivable, is of central importance.

THE BENEFIT OF OTHERS

The Lord Buddha said, "So, Subhūti, these bodhisattvas, great beings, practise for the benefit of many people. They want to be completely enlightened in supreme, truly perfect enlightenment for the happiness of many people, out of sympathy for the world, for the advantage of a great body of people, for their benefit, for their happiness, with sympathy for gods and for men who need sympathy. Once they have been completely enlightened in supreme, truly perfect enlightenment, then they want to explain the teaching."

Subhūti asked, "Lord Buddha, how does a bodhisattva, a great being, acting here in the perfection of wisdom, come to fulfil the development of the perfection of wisdom?"

The Lord Buddha replied, "When a bodhisattva, a great being, acts in the perfection of wisdom, he does not see an increase in form, Subhūti, as he acts in the perfection of wisdom. And thus, as he acts in the perfection of wisdom, he sees neither an increase in feeling, nor in perception, nor in mental activities, nor in consciousness. As he acts in the perfection of wisdom, he does not see a decrease in form. And thus, as he acts in the perfection of wisdom, he sees neither a decrease in feeling, nor in perception, nor in mental activities, nor in consciousness. He does not see any phenomenon, as he acts in the perfection of wisdom. He does not see no phenomenon either, as he acts in the perfection of wisdom. So he comes to fulfil the development of the perfection of wisdom."

Subhūti said, "You are explaining the inconceivable!" [219]

In Buddhism, time operates in vast periodic cycles of universal evolution and disintegration. Some of these cycles are times when a Buddha teaches, some are not. We are fortunate to be in a cycle when Buddhas teach, and in a time when the teachings of an historical Buddha are well-known. The teachings arise and are "as new as fresh cream". Over centuries they spread around the world, until the period of disintegration when they finally disappear. The prediction is that the final flourish of the teachings of the present Buddha will be somewhere to the North …

PREDICTIONS OF THE SPREAD OF THE TEACHINGS

"Moreover, after the passing away of the Tathāgata, these sūtras associated with the six perfections will spread in the South. Then they will spread from the South to the East, and then they will spread from the East to the North. Śāriputra, the Tathāgata focuses on these, when training in the teachings is as new as fresh cream, until the period of time when the true teaching disappears. During this time, worthy sons and worthy daughters will set out this perfection of wisdom. They will preserve it, they will discuss it, they will study it and they will be intent on it. They will explain it, they will advise on it, they will instruct in it, and they will recite it well. Writing it out accordingly, producing books about it, they will preserve it. Śāriputra, the Tathāgata knows them. Śāriputra, the Tathāgata sustains them. Śāriputra, the Tathāgata sees them. Śāriputra, the Tathāgata looks upon them with the eye of a Buddha."

Śāriputra said, "So, Lord Buddha, will this deep perfection of wisdom be widespread in the final time, during the last period, in the North, in the northern region?"

The Lord Buddha replied, "Those in the North, in the northern region, hearing about the deep perfection of wisdom here, will make an effort in this perfection of wisdom and they will make it widespread." [225-226]

Māra is the mythological personification of all evils and passions, the arch rival of the Buddha. His teachings are false and misleading, he creates discord and discourages effort, he distracts and frightens. Māra takes pleasure in keeping bodhisattvas from enlightenment and he relishes suffering.

How Māra Diverts Bodhisattvas from the Perfection of Wisdom

"Moreover, Subhūti, when this deep perfection of wisdom is being described, explained, advised on, instructed in, set out, discussed, recited well, and then written down accordingly, much clever wit can arise which causes distraction of thought. This should be known as the work of Māra against these bodhisattvas, great beings."

So then the venerable Subhūti said to the Lord Buddha, "But, Lord Buddha, it is possible to write down the perfection of wisdom."

The Lord Buddha replied, "Not at all, Subhūti! Whoever thinks, Subhūti, after writing down the letters of the words in the perfection of wisdom, 'The perfection of wisdom is written' will also come to think, 'That is not true'. They will devote their attention to the perfection of wisdom as words, or not as words. This too, Subhūti, should be known as the work of Māra against them.

"Moreover, Subhūti, when this perfection of wisdom is being written down, they may be diverted. Places — a village, a town, a

settlement, the country, a kingdom, or a garden may divert
attention. A guru, a legend, or a thief may divert attention. Steps
leading down to a river, streets, or a palanquin may divert attention.
Happiness, suffering, or fear may divert attention. A woman, a man,
or a hermaphrodite may divert attention. Confused situations may
divert attention. Relationships with mothers and fathers, with
brothers and sisters, with friends, acquaintances, mother's relatives
and father's relatives, with a wife, a son, or a daughter may divert
attention. Relationships with home, food, and drink may divert

attention. Clothes, bed, necessities, obligation, greed, hate, delusion, opportunity, good times, bad times, songs, musical instruments, dance, poetry, plays and legends, treatises, business, jokes, musical shows, sorrow, trouble, and the self may divert attention. These and other diversions, Subhūti, are arranged by the evil Māra ... " [240-241]

In traditional Indian cosmology, the realm of desire (kāmādhātu) includes this world, while the realm of form (rūpādhātu), where the inhabitants, though corporeal, do not suffer from sensual desire, includes the god Brahmā's world. There is also a further realm, a formless realm (ārūpyadhātu), where there is neither form nor sensual desire.

The Gods

The Lord Buddha addressed the gods dwelling in the realm of desire and the gods dwelling in the realm of form, saying, "If, gods, any worthy son or worthy daughter should hear this deep perfection of wisdom, it follows, gods, that they should expect nirvāṇa more quickly than those who practised for an aeon, or for what is left of an aeon, at the stage of following faithfully."

Then the gods dwelling in the realm of desire and the gods dwelling in the realm of form said to the Lord Buddha, "This perfection of wisdom is a great perfection!" After saying that, they bowed at the feet of the Lord Buddha. They circumambulated the Lord Buddha three times and then set off, after announcing, "We will now leave the presence of the Lord Buddha." After going a little way, they vanished – the gods dwelling in the realm of desire departed to the realm of desire and the gods dwelling in the realm of form departed to Brahma's world. [283]

61

THE SIMILE OF THE SHIP

"When a ship is wrecked at sea, those who do not hold onto a timber, or plank, or other solid support will drown in the water, never reaching the shore. Subhūti, those that do hold onto a timber, or plank, or other solid support will not drown in the water. Happily unhindered, they may reach the shore, where they will stand safe and sound on firm ground.

"Similarly, Subhūti, a bodhisattva who is endowed with a full measure of faith and purity, of kindness and intentions, but without taking hold of the perfection of wisdom, can fall along the way. Not reaching all-embracing knowledge, he may remain only a disciple, or a pratyekabuddha." [286]

Dependent origination is an interlinked series of conditions; an explanation of the suffering that keeps us bound to the cycle of rebirths. Decay and dying exist through the condition of birth, birth through the condition of becoming, becoming through the condition of grasping, grasping through the condition of craving, craving through the condition of feelings, feelings through the condition of contact, contact through the condition of the sense fields, the sense fields through the condition of name and form, name and form through the condition of consciousness, consciousness through the condition of mental activities, and mental activities through the condition of ignorance.

A Buddha shows a path which leads to the stopping of suffering. It is this path which a bodhisattva follows, analyzing dependent origination and devoting himself to others, until he reaches a stage where he is irreversible; broken free from dependent origination.

How Should a Bodhisattva Behave?

Venerable Subhūti asked the Lord Buddha, "How, Lord Buddha, should a bodhisattva, a great being, who wants to go forth to supreme, truly perfect enlightenment, behave? How should he be instructed?"

The Lord Buddha replied, "Subhūti, a bodhisattva, a great being, who wants to go forth to supreme, truly perfect enlightenment, should behave equally to all sentient beings. He should produce

thoughts that are fair to all sentient beings. He should handle
others with thoughts that are impartial, that are friendly, that are
favourable, that are helpful. He should handle others with thoughts
that are non-confrontational, that avoid harm, that avoid hurt, that
avoid distress. He should handle others, all sentient beings, using
the understanding of a mother, using the understanding of a father,
the understanding of a son and the understanding of a daughter.
So, Subhūti, a bodhisattva, a great being, who wants to be completely
enlightened in supreme, truly perfect enlightenment should stand

alongside all sentient beings. For so he should be trained to be the refuge of all sentient beings. In his own behaviour he should renounce all evil. He should give gifts, he should guard morality, he should exercise patience, he should exert vigour, he should enter into contemplation, and he should master this wisdom! He should consider dependent origination backwards and forwards and he should instigate, encourage and empower that in others." [321-322]

WHAT IS AN IRREVERSIBLE BODHISATTVA?

"He does not talk meaninglessly about anything at all. He has something to say only when it has a purpose, and not when it has no purpose. He does not judge what others have done or have not done. Subhūti, because of these aspects, these signs, these reasons, a bodhisattva, a great being, should be understood as irreversible from supreme, truly perfect enlightenment." [323]

TEN PATHS OF GOOD ACTION

"Furthermore, Subhūti, an irreversible bodhisattva, a great being, undertakes to observe the ten paths of good action. He abstains from, and encourages others to abstain from killing. He abstains from, and encourages others to abstain from taking what has not been given. He abstains from, and encourages others to abstain from sexual misconduct. He abstains from, and encourages others to abstain from wine, beer, spirits, and other intoxicants. He abstains from, and encourages others to abstain from telling lies. He abstains from, and encourages others to abstain from malicious speech. He abstains from, and encourages others to abstain from harsh speech. He abstains from, and encourages others to abstain from slander. He abstains from, and encourages others to abstain from covetousness. He abstains from, and encourages others to abstain from ill will. He abstains from, and encourages others to abstain from wrong views.

"Thus, Subhūti, an irreversible bodhisattva, a great being, personally undertakes to observe the ten paths of good action. He also shows others the ten paths of good action. He encourages, he enthuses, he inspires, he establishes, he is committed. Even when he is dreaming, he does not commit offences against the ten paths of good action, neither once, nor many times, nor in any way at all, nor at any time, never. He does not even think of it. Even when he is dreaming, Subhūti, an irreversible bodhisattva, a great being, keeps in mind the ten paths of good action. A bodhisattva, a great being, endowed with these aspects, with these signs, for these reasons, should be understood as irreversible from supreme, truly perfect enlightenment." [324-325]

PURIFICATION OF THOUGHT

The Lord Buddha said, "Subhūti, as the roots of virtue of that bodhisattva, a great being, increase, that bodhisattva is occupied in his thoughts with few cares. He is occupied with thoughts that are free from treachery, with thoughts that are free from deceit, with thoughts that are free from crookedness and with thoughts that are free from craftiness. And, Subhūti, by the purification of thought, he goes beyond the stage of disciples and pratyekabuddhas. It is this, Subhūti, which should be understood as the purification of thought of that bodhisattva, a great being. Subhūti, an irreversible bodhisattva, a great being, endowed with these aspects, these characteristics, these distinctive features, will keep in mind supreme, truly perfect enlightenment.

"Moreover, Subhūti, an irreversible bodhisattva, a great being, is not one to give weight to gain, honour and fame. He is not one to give weight to fancy robes, a fine alms bowl, a nice dwelling place or impressive medical instruments. He is not full of envy and meanness. When deep things are described, he is not discouraged. His understanding becomes sustained. His understanding is deep. He eagerly hears teaching from others, and he incorporates all that teaching into the perfection of wisdom. He incorporates all the worldly arts and professions through their inherent nature, thanks to the perfection of wisdom. There is no phenomenon which he does not see as tied to the sphere of phenomena, everything is seen as being tied to that. An irreversible bodhisattva, a great being, endowed with these aspects, these characteristics, these distinctive features, will keep in mind supreme, truly perfect enlightenment."
[327]

The Word of Māra

"Furthermore, Subhūti, the evil Māra, appearing in the disguise of a monk, approaches a bodhisattva, a great being, and says, 'Consider what you heard before, and reject what you accepted then. If you consider it, you will reject it. So, we will repeatedly try to persuade you. What you have heard up to now is not the word of a Buddha – it is just poetry, made up by poets. But what I say is what the Buddha spoke. This is the word of the Buddha.' Subhūti, if a bodhisattva, after hearing this, is shaken or diverted, it should be understood that this is not a bodhisattva as predicted by the Tathāgatas, and that this bodhisattva does not conform to essential irreversibility from supreme, truly perfect enlightenment." [328-329]

The Simile of Lust

"Subhūti, any man may act from desire, expecting things. That man, acting from desire, expecting things, may arrange a rendezvous with a beautiful, attractive and good-looking woman. But others may restrict that woman. She may be forbidden to leave her house alone. What do you think of that, Subhūti? What are the rising expectations of that man focused upon?"

Subhūti replied, "The rising expectations of that man are focused upon the woman! He fantasizes, 'If she comes, when she comes,

I will be intimate with her, I will ravish her, I will play erotically with her, I will make love with her'."

The Lord Buddha asked, "What do you think of that, Subhūti? How often may the expectations of that man rise in the course of a day?"

Subhūti replied, "Lord Buddha, in the course of a day, the expectations of that man will rise many times!"

The Lord Buddha said, "Subhūti, a bodhisattva, a great being, clears away, cuts short and puts an end to aeons of saṃsāra, as many in number as the rising expectations of that man in the course of a day." [343]

The simile of the lamp is often used to explain the production of the thought of enlightenment in its relationship with dependent origination – the chain of cause and effect that ties us to existence (saṃsāra). Like all phenomena, the wick and the flame of an oil lamp exist only in their relationship to other things. The flame depends on the wick; when the wick is totally burnt up, the flame will die out. The cause of this burning up of the wick cannot be pinned down to the first time that the flame touches the wick, or to the last time, or to any moment in between. This illustrates that nothing has an unchanging nature, nothing exists independently; everything is tied together by dependent origination.

Subhūti queries how it is possible to analyze the process of enlightenment, when nothing, including that process, including the thought of enlightenment, exists in absolute terms, but only in its relationship to everything else. The only answer is to continue to use terms of reference that have no absolute existence, but which are necessary if we are to function at all in a world that we do not fully understand.

THE SIMILE OF THE LAMP

Then the venerable Subhūti said to the Lord Buddha, "When a bodhisattva, a great being, becomes completely enlightened in supreme, truly perfect enlightenment, is this due to the production of the first thought or ... is this due to the production of the last thought? Lord Buddha, the previous production of thought is not inextricably linked with the last production of thought, and the last production of thought is not inextricably linked with the previous production of thought. How, Lord Buddha, does a bodhisattva, a great being, accumulate the roots of virtue?"

The Lord Buddha replied to the venerable Subhūti, "What do you think about that, Subhūti? In the burning of an oil lamp, does the flame burn the wick by its first contact, or does the flame burn the wick by its last contact?"

Subhūti replied, "Neither, Lord Buddha. Because, Lord Buddha, the flame neither burns up the wick by its first contact, nor ... when it is no longer in first contact. Lord Buddha, the flame does not burn up the wick by its last contact, nor ... when it is no longer in last contact."

The Lord Buddha asked, "What do you think about that, Subhūti? Is the wick definitely burned?"

Subhūti replied, "It is burned, Lord Buddha. It is burned, Sugata."

The Lord Buddha said, "And similarly, Subhūti, a bodhisattva, a great being, does not become completely enlightened in supreme, truly perfect enlightenment by the production of the first thought, nor ... when there is no longer the production of the first thought. And a bodhisattva, a great being, does not become completely enlightened in supreme, truly perfect enlightenment by the production of the last thought, nor ... when there is no longer the production of the last thought. He becomes completely enlightened not from the production of these thoughts and not other than from the production of these thoughts. And yet a bodhisattva, a great being, does become completely enlightened in supreme, truly perfect enlightenment."[352-353]

Maitreya, addressed as Ajita, is the next future Buddha. To be reborn in his time is considered especially fortunate, and he is expected to have many more followers than the present Buddha. Maitreya does not often speak, but he is even now an important figure, very advanced in his thought. His role in the perfection of wisdom literature is to expound the most obscure of metaphysical matters.

Maitreya shows that analysis of phenomena has no real substance. Ultimately, analysis is only words, amounting to nothing in absolute terms. He also points to the danger of being paralysed by philosophical analysis; but if one accepts the voidness of all existence, it does not mean that one cannot still follow the practical path outlined by the Buddha, here the path of the six perfections.

MAITREYA ON THE PERFECTION OF WISDOM

Subhūti said, "Venerable Śāriputra, Maitreya, a bodhisattva, and a very great being, is present. The Tathāgata has predicted his supreme, truly perfect enlightenment. In this matter he is an eye-witness, one should question him on this, and he will reply about the matter."

Then the venerable Śāriputra said to Maitreya, "Venerable Maitreya, Subhūti the Elder has said, 'This is Maitreya, a bodhisattva, a great being. He will reply on this matter.' Reply accordingly on the matter, venerable Ajita!"

Then Maitreya said to the venerable Subhūti, "When the venerable Subhūti said, 'This is Maitreya, a bodhisattva, a great being, he will reply on this matter', what is this name 'Maitreya', what does 'he will reply on this matter' mean? Does my form reply? Do feeling, perception, mental activities, or even consciousness reply? Does my appearance or my shape reply? Does the voidness of form reply? Does the voidness of feeling, perception, mental activities, or consciousness reply? Does the voidness of my appearance or my shape reply?

"But, venerable Subhūti, the voidness of form cannot reply. So, venerable Subhūti, the voidness of feeling, perception, mental activities or consciousness, and the voidness of my appearance or my shape cannot reply? Venerable Subhūti, I do not see any phenomenon that could reply, or that should reply, or by which there could be a reply. I do not see any phenomenon which was predicted as supreme, truly perfect enlightenment."

Then the venerable Śāriputra said to Maitreya, a bodhisattva, a great being, "But, venerable Maitreya, have you experienced these phenomena which you speak about?"

Maitreya replied, "Venerable Śāriputra, I have not experienced these phenomena which I speak about. Thus, venerable Śāriputra, as I speak about these phenomena, I do not know them, nor do I think about them, nor apperceive them, nor see them. And also, venerable Subhūti, form cannot touch them, words cannot express them, mind cannot consider them. That is their intrinsic nature, because they have no intrinsic nature!"

Then the venerable Śāriputra said, "There is deep wisdom in what Maitreya has said. Indeed, he explains things as someone who has acted in the perfection of wisdom for a long time."

Then the Lord Buddha said to the venerable Śāriputra, "Where, Śāriputra, did that, 'There is deep wisdom in what Maitreya has said' come from? Śāriputra, can you see the phenomenon that brought about your becoming an arhat?"

Śāriputra replied, "Not at all, Lord Buddha!"

The Lord Buddha said, "Similarly, a bodhisattva, a great being, acting in the perfection of wisdom, does not think, 'This phenomenon has been predicted, is predicted, was predicted and is completely understood in supreme, truly perfect enlightenment.' Acting thus, a bodhisattva, a great being, acts in the perfection of wisdom. Acting, he is not nervous, he is not frightened, he is not terrified. Imbued with the strength that he has gained, he thinks, 'I am not yet fully enlightened' and therefore he makes more effort. And so, when he acts, he acts in the perfection of wisdom." [359-361]

A SMILE OF RECOGNITION

There was a woman who had come to that assembly, and sat down. She rose from her seat, adjusted her top robe over one shoulder, knelt to the earth on her right knee, folded her hands towards the Lord Buddha, and said to him, "Lord Buddha, in this place I am not frightened, I am not terrified. Not trembling, not frightened, and not terrified, I will show the teachings to all sentient beings."

Then the Lord Buddha broke into a smile, golden in colour on that occasion. By its lustre, it beamed through endless and boundless world systems, rising up as far as Brahmā's world. Then, after it returned, it circled around the Lord Buddha three times, and then finally faded from his face. Immediately after the Lord Buddha had

broken into that smile, the woman seized some golden flowers, strewing and scattering the golden flowers over the Lord Buddha. But then those golden flowers, unsupported, were suspended in the air!

Then the venerable Ānanda rose from his seat, adjusted his top robe over one shoulder, knelt to the earth on his right knee, folded his hands towards the Lord Buddha, and said to him, "What prompted that, Lord Buddha? What was the reason you broke into a smile? Truly perfectly enlightened Tathāgatas and arhats do not break into a smile without cause or good reason."

So then the Lord Buddha replied to the venerable Ānanda, "Ānanda, this is our sister, the goddess of the Ganges! In a future time she will be the Tathāgata called 'Golden Flower'. She will arise as an arhat, truly perfectly enlightened, accomplished in knowledge and good conduct, a Sugata, street-wise, supreme, a tamer of wild men, a teacher of both gods and men, a Buddha, a Lord Buddha. She will become completely enlightened in supreme, truly perfect enlightenment in the stellar aeon." [365-367]

Good friends (kalyāṇamitra) are regarded as indispensable for the help and support they can give spiritually. A good friend is an important factor in the attainment of the thought of enlightenment. The friend should be intelligent, with sensible views, high ideals and faith, and will help a bodhisattva to be fearless and courageous. A poor friend, by not warning against errors and inferior ideals, might lead a bodhisattva from the perfections. The Buddhas will also prove good friends, as will the perfections themselves.

Good Friends

"Subhūti, a bodhisattva, a great being, who has set out with earnest intention and wants to reach supreme, truly perfect enlightenment, should from the very beginning tend, love and honour good friends."

Subhūti asked, "Lord Buddha, who are these good friends of a bodhisattva … ?"

The Lord Buddha replied, "Subhūti, they are the Lord Buddhas, the irreversible bodhisattvas, the great beings who are skilful in bodhisattva practice, who instruct and advise him in the perfections, and who demonstrate and show the perfection of wisdom. Subhūti, these are meant to be the good friends of a bodhisattva. The perfection of wisdom in particular should be regarded as a good friend of a bodhisattva, a great being.

"In fact, all the six perfections are meant to be the good friends of a bodhisattva, a great being. The six perfections are the path and the light, the six perfections are a meteor, an illumination, a shelter, a home, a goal, an island, a mother and a father, the six perfections lead to knowledge, to understanding, to supreme, truly perfect enlightenment.

"Why? Subhūti, the perfection of wisdom, that is to say the six perfections, is taught thoroughly. Subhūti, in past times the Tathāgatas, then arhats, became truly perfectly enlightened, liberated in complete enlightenment, in the supreme, truly perfect enlightenment of these Lord Buddhas. All-embracing knowledge, that is to say the six perfections, is made visible." [396-397]

Karma, or actions, have a significant effect in this life and on future births. A bodhisattva's compassion stems from his awareness that the effect of karma is continuous, carrying over into future lives.

GREAT COMPASSION

"Subhūti, someone endowed with that sort of wisdom is a bodhisattva, a great being. But he sees that all sentient beings, even those endowed with great wisdom, are condemned to die. And at that point he is seized with great compassion. Surveying with a celestial eye countless, innumerable, immeasurable, unlimited sentient beings, he sees that they are endowed with continuous karma. He sees them acquiring unfortunate rebirths, doomed to death, entangled in a net of false views, not finding a path, never again acquiring a fortunate rebirth. He sees them losing out on fortunate rebirths, and at that point he is greatly agitated. Then, with his great friendliness for all sentient beings, beaming with great compassion, he gives them his attention and he vows, 'I will be the refuge for all these sentient beings. I will bring about release from all suffering for these sentient beings.'" [402-403]

THE SIMILE OF THE LOST JEWELS

"Subhūti, suppose a man, knowledgeable about fabulous jewels, had acquired a priceless, fabulous jewel, a fabulous jewel of a kind he knew of but had not previously acquired. Acquiring that jewel would give him much intense pleasure and delight. But if he lost that jewel of his, for that reason he would be burdened with great distress. His attention would constantly turn to focus upon that

jewel, thinking, 'Oh dear, now I've lost that priceless, fabulous jewel!' Thinking this, that man would not forget for a moment his priceless, fabulous jewel until he had acquired another jewel of the same quality and kind. Similarly, Subhūti, a bodhisattva, a great being, could lose the priceless, fabulous jewel of the perfection of wisdom. The jewel being lost, but still having the idea of a priceless, fabulous jewel, his attention would be diverted from the perfection of wisdom. His attention to the perfection of wisdom abandoned, he then searches with the thought of all-embracing knowledge until he acquires something equivalent. All that time he should never have abandoned his attention focused on acquiring the priceless, fabulous jewel of the perfection of wisdom and the priceless, fabulous jewel of all-embracing knowledge." [404-405]

MĀRA

Ānanda asked, "What sort of bodhisattva does evil Māra intend to harm?"

The Lord Buddha replied, "Ānanda, evil Māra appears, intending to harm a bodhisattva, a great being, who in the past did not think he was interested when the perfection of wisdom was being taught. Also, Ānanda, evil Māra appears, intending to harm a bodhisattva, a great being, who, when this profundity, this perfection of wisdom, is being taught, is full of doubts, sceptical, thinking that perhaps this perfection of wisdom is true, perhaps it is not. Furthermore, Ānanda, evil Māra appears, intending to harm a bodhisattva who lacks a good spiritual friend, who is influenced by bad friends, and who, when the perfection of wisdom is being taught, does not take in the very deep points. He is ignorant and does not know. Unknowing, he does not ask how to develop the perfection of wisdom. Also, Ānanda, evil Māra appears, intending to harm a bodhisattva who clings to someone upholding a false teaching and says, 'I am his follower and he will not abandon me in any situation. There are many other bodhisattvas whom I might follow, but they do not appeal to me. I have taken this one as my fitting companion and he will suit me.'

"Furthermore, Ānanda, a bodhisattva, a great being, when this profundity, this perfection of wisdom, is being taught, may say to another bodhisattva, 'This perfection of wisdom is indeed profound, but what point is there in listening to it? For even if I dedicate myself to what the Tathāgata has taught in other texts, I do not get to the bottom of it, nor derive any enjoyment from it. What is the point of listening to it and reciting it?' In this way, he tries to mislead other bodhisattvas. So, Ānanda, evil Māra appears, intending to harm a bodhisattva, a great being." [417-418]

Pleasing Māra

"The evil Māra was pleased, excited, enraptured, delighted, and filled with joy and gladness.

"Moreover, Ānanda, when a bodhisattva fights a person belonging to the vehicle of the disciples (Śravakayāna), when he disputes with him, quarrels with him, abuses him, reviles him, shows malice to him and incites hatred, then he is entirely in the hands of the evil Māra, who thinks, 'Ah, this worthy son will turn away from all-embracing knowledge and will remain far from all-embracing knowledge.' And Māra becomes more and more pleased if a person belonging to the bodhisattva vehicle fights with another person belonging to the bodhisattva vehicle, if he disputes with him, quarrels with him, abuses him, reviles him, shows malice to him and incites hatred. He becomes excited, enraptured, delighted, and filled with joy and gladness. And so the two of them are in his hands and both these bodhisattvas will remain far from all-embracing knowledge.

"Moreover, Ānanda, a predicted bodhisattva, a great being, might fight with an unpredicted bodhisattva, a great being. He might dispute with him, might quarrel with him, might abuse him, might revile him, might show malice to him, and might incite hatred. The thought then occurs to that bodhisattva, a great being, that he would have been armed with armour for an aeon, if he had not abandoned all-embracing knowledge." [420]

THE SIMILE OF SPACE

"Lord Buddha, space does not think, 'What am I near to, what am I far from?' Why? Because, Lord Buddha, space does not make such discriminations. Similarly, Lord Buddha, a bodhisattva, a great being, practising the perfection of wisdom, does not think, 'I am near supreme, truly perfect enlightenment, I am far from the stage of a disciple or the stage of a pratyekabuddha.' Why? Because the perfection of wisdom is something free from such discriminations." [441]

BEYOND MEASURE

"The perfection of wisdom has no limit, Ānanda. The perfection of wisdom is inexhaustible. The perfection of wisdom has no end. Why? Because these do not apply to the perfection of wisdom. For someone to think that a limit, exhaustion or end could be attributed to the perfection of wisdom would be like attributing a limit, exhaustion or end to space. Why? Because the perfection of wisdom has no limit, Ānanda. Because the perfection of wisdom is inexhaustible. Because the perfection of wisdom has no end. I've said that there is no limit, exhaustion or end to the perfection of wisdom. A mass of words, a mass of sentences, a mass of syllables, Ānanda, that is bound by a limit, but this perfection of wisdom is bound by no limit. Why? Ānanda, the perfection of wisdom is not just a mass of words, or a mass of sentences, or a mass of syllables! Ānanda, the perfection of wisdom is beyond measure!" [466-467]

Ānanda was either in attendance for all of the Buddha's teachings, or had reports of them directly from the Buddha. At the First Council after the Buddha's death, it was Ānanda who first recited the teachings as he recalled them, establishing an agreed canon of texts. That assembly met for several months at Rājagrha, not far from the Vulture Peak.

ĀNANDA'S TEACHER DEPARTS

The Lord Buddha took his leave of the venerable Ānanda, saying, "You should understand the perfection of wisdom in this way, and having absorbed that, consume the all-embracing knowledge of the bodhisattvas, great beings. Therefore, Ānanda, bodhisattvas, great beings, who want to acquire all-embracing knowledge should then practise in this perfection of wisdom. They should listen to it and they should take it up. They should preserve it, discuss it, and study it. They should explain it, advise on it, and instruct in it. They should recite it well and write it out. Having put it in a great book, well written, in the clearest of words, on the authority of the Tathāgata, it

should be honoured, adored, respected, revered, paid homage to, and esteemed, with flowers, incense, perfumes, garlands, oils, powders, robes, music, clothes, parasols, banners, bells, and flags, with rows of lamps all around, with reverence in every way imaginable. This is our advice to you, Ānanda. Why? Because this is the way the full development of all-embracing knowledge in the perfection of wisdom will be brought about. What do you think about that, Ānanda? Is the Tathāgata your teacher?"

Ānanda replied, "That is my teacher, Lord Buddha. That is my teacher, Sugata."

So then the Lord Buddha said to the venerable Ānanda, "The Tathāgata is your teacher, Ānanda. I've been well served by your charming, kind gestures, words and thoughts. In that case, Ānanda, just as you now have given me affection, faith, and respect, remaining with me, living with me, spending time with me in this incarnation, so, Ānanda, after my death you should act similarly towards this perfection of wisdom, time and time again. To you, Ānanda, I present, I pass on this perfection of wisdom, so that it will not simply vanish! No other man could be more suitable than you. Ānanda, it should be understood that as long as this perfection of wisdom circulates in the world, the Tathāgata in a sense remains. It should be understood that in a sense, the Tathāgata continues to explain his teaching. And, Ānanda, it should be understood that sentient beings have not been deserted, they have the vision of the Buddha, they can hear his teachings, and they can take part in his religious community. Ānanda, it should be understood that these sentient beings remain close to the Tathāgata. They can listen to the perfection of wisdom and they can take it up. They can preserve it, discuss it, study it, and be intent on it. They can explain it, advise on it, and instruct in it. They can recite it well and write it out. They can honour, adore, respect, revere, pay homage to, and esteem the perfection of wisdom, with flowers, incense, perfumes, garlands, oils, powders, robes, parasols, banners, bells, and flags, with rows of lamps all around, with reverence in every way imaginable." [527-528]

About the Illustrations

front endpapers: Add.1464, f.227r, *lp*. A yellow Tārā making the gesture of giving (varada mudrā), probably holding a lotus. A green Tārā on the right seems to be offering a lotus. Nothing is clear due to the condition of the illustration.

p.5: Add.1643, *cover detail*. Prajñāpāramitā, personification of the perfection of wisdom, on a lotus throne. She holds a rosary and a book, and two hands are in the gesture of teaching (dharmacakra mudrā). The wooden cover is of a later date than the manuscript, probably late 11th-century.

p.13: Add.1464, f.127v, *cp detail*. The first teaching of the historical Buddha in the Deer Park at Sārnāth (eastern Uttar Pradesh). The central figure is the Buddha making the gesture of teaching. Two disciples, probably Śāriputra and Maudgalyāyana, honour the Buddha (cf. p.103). At the front of the lotus throne, but not shown here, is a wheel of the law (dharmacakra) and two deer.

p.15: Add.1643, f.200v, *lp detail*. A yellow Vasudhārā, goddess of wealth, in a temple in Kāñcīpuram (northern Tamilnadu). She is making the gestures of giving and remembering the Buddha (buddhasmaraṇa mudrā), and holds a jewel, a book, a stalk and a lotus. She rewards those who honour her – here each attendant has a full golden dish.

p.17: Add.1643, f.74v, *lp*. The historical Buddha seated European style under a tree, making the gesture of teaching to five bodhisattvas – a green Samantabhadra, a blue Vajrapāṇi, a yellow Maitreya, a yellow Mañjuśrī and a white Avalokiteśvara. To the right, a wrathful yellow Jambhala holds his mongoose and makes the gesture of giving. Above his head are two birds.

p.18: Add.1464, f. 226v, *rp*. A green Tārā making the gesture of giving and probably holding a lotus. She has two attendants: a yellow Mārīcī and, presumably, a blue Ekajaṭā.

p.21: Add.1464, f.227r, *cp*. A white Siṃhanāda Avalokiteśvara bare of all jewellery, seated on a lion. His right leg is held in position by a meditation cord (rājalīlāsana). An uncoloured lotus is on the right.

p.23: Add.1643, f.127r, *rp*. The ornate Aśokan stūpa at Rāḍhya (northern Bihār). To the right is a monastery, with a monk seated on the veranda. On the far left is a victory pillar (jayastambha), surmounted by an aroused garuḍa, the half-human king of the birds (cf. p.29). The pillar can be visited to this day, though the distinctive top has not survived. Both monk and bird are making a gesture of honouring (namaskāra mudrā). A curtain and garlands hang from the sky.

p.26: Add.1643, f.222r, *cp*. A lotus flower. Lotus symbols permeate Buddhism in general and the illustrations of this text

in particular. The lotus flower is always pure, no matter how unclean the water in which it grows – a natural analogy for bodhisattva practice and worldly existence.

p.29: Add.1643, f.216v, *rp*. The Candrana monastery at Supācanagara (founded by the sage Vulbhuka), with a monk on the veranda. There is a stūpa and a victory pillar surmounted by an elephant (cf. p.23). Two monks seem to be in conversation.

p.30: Add.1643, f.176v, *rp*. Stūpa in the Deer Park at Vārendrā (northwestern Bangladesh). It has six terraces in the form of a lotus, and a cupola with a parasol and banners blowing in the wind. There is a Buddha in the open niche of the cupola. Two monks, wearing thin, clinging tunics and mantles, revere the stūpa at night.

p.32: Add.1643, f.40v, *lp*. A white Avalokiteśvara in Magadha (central Bihār), making the gesture of giving and holding a lotus. He is attended by a green Tārā, a yellow Prince Sudhana, a red Hayagrīva and a yellow Bhṛkuṭi, who is holding a book.

p.35: Add.1464, f.127v, *lp*. The historical Buddha seated under a tree in the mango grove at Vaiśali (northern Bihār). He holds a begging bowl full of honey, collected by the monkeys. In the sky there is a deity (devatā). (Cf. p.52.)

p.36: Add.1464, f.226v, *cp*. The Buddha's death and entry into final nirvāṇa (parinirvāṇa) at Kuśinagara (eastern Uttar Pradesh). He is accompanied by two monks.

p.39: Add.1643, f.151r, *lp detail*. A white Avalokiteśvara with attendant, in a temple at Konkan (Maharashtra). He is making the gesture of giving and holds a lotus. On the right, a red Mārīcī makes the gesture of remembering the Buddha.

p.41: Add.1643, f.179v, *rp*. A white Avalokiteśvara at Vedakota in Koratra, making the gesture of giving and holding a lotus. He is honoured by two bodhisattva attendants, perhaps a Mārīcī and a Tārā. The third attendant is Hayagrīva. He holds a club and wears a flaming head-dress, a green horse's head and many earrings, necklaces, bracelets and anklets.

p.42: Add.1643, f.120r, *rp*. A green Tārā in Kamboja (northern Pakistan), making the gesture of giving and holding a lotus. She is attended by a yellow Mārīcī making the gesture of reassurance (abhaya mudrā) and holding a lotus in full bloom, and by a blue Ekajaṭā making the gesture of explanation (vitarka mudrā) with her right hand and the gesture of knowledge (jñāna mudrā) with her left.

p.45: Add.1464, f.128r, *lp*. The Buddha calming the mad elephant Nālāgiri at Rājagṛha (central Bihār). The elephant is shown enraged and then calmed, and the fear of the two disciples is vividly depicted as they cling like children to the Buddha. He is making the gesture of reassurance and, with his left hand, the gesture of explanation. His left hand is reflected off to the right as fire (tejas), the essence of spiritual power. Springing from the fingers of his right hand are five lions.

p.46: Add.1643, f.222r, *rp*. The Buddha at Bodhgayā (central Bihār) calling the earth to witness (bhūmisparśa mudrā) under the bodhi tree (cf. p.59). He has a halo behind him and his left hand is in the gesture of meditation (dhyāna mudrā).

p.48: Add.1643, f.169r, *lp*. An ornate stūpa in Oḍradeśa (northern Orissa). Its parasol appears to be floating miraculously in the air (presumably it is attached to the cave ceiling). A monk honours the stūpa. To the left, there are four bodhisattvas – possibly a red Amitabha, a green Samantabhadra, a yellow Maitreya and a blue Vajrapāṇī. Two stūpas are in the background. There is a border of stones at the front, and a balustrade is on the left.

p.51: Add.1643, f.127r, *lp*. A green Samantabhadra in China, sitting astride his elephant. He is making the gesture of teaching and holding a golden sceptre. Trees and mountains are in the background.

p.52: Add.1643, f.157v, *lp*. A green Tārā making the gesture of giving and holding a lotus. With her in the temple is an attendant, probably Ekajaṭā. On the left, the historical Buddha is seated European style under a tree at Vaiśali (northern Bihār). He holds a begging bowl full of honey, given to him by the monkeys. A monkey is approaching with a bowl of honey. In the sky there is a deity. (Cf. p.35.)

p.55: Add.1643, f.214v, *rp*. The ornate Rhinoceros Horn stūpa (khaḍga caitya) on the Black Mountain in Konkan (a rhinoceros horn is the symbol of the solitary pratyekabuddha). The stūpa is bordered by cave temple walls and monks' cells are carved among the rocks. Three monks make gestures of honouring and a fourth holds a book. These are probably the famous Kanheri Caves, north of Bombay, where many small cave cells and the remains of several stūpas can be seen.

p.56: Add.1464, f.127v, *rp*. Queen Māyā, after giving birth to the historical Buddha. She stands under a sal tree in the Lumbinī grove (southern Nepal), supported by her sister. The child was born from her right side and is portrayed to the left as a miniature Buddha. The seven steps he took at birth are represented on the ground. Indra, wearing a three-crested crown, offers a cloth to the Buddha.

p.59: Add.1464, f.2r, *cp*. The historical Buddha calls the earth to witness at Bodhgayā (central Bihār) with an earthquake (cf. p.46). Māra, in the form of the god of desire Kāma, shoots an arrow at the Buddha, while his beautiful daughters attempt to distract the Buddha's attention.

p.60: Add.1464, f.128r, *rp*. The historical Buddha at Sāmkaśya (western Uttar Pradesh), after descending from heaven where he had been teaching his deceased mother. His right hand is making the gesture of giving, his left the gesture of explanation. Brahmā, representing gods from the realm of form, is on the left; Indra, representing gods from the realm of desire, is on the right. Both are honouring the Buddha. A stūpa is in the upper left.

p.63: Add.1643, f.20v, *lp*. The Buddha of the past, Dīpaṃkara (cf. p.83), at sea with two attendant bodhisattvas in canopied boats. Shellfish, a tortoise, fish, a horse with wings, a makara and the head of Rāhu are in the water. Curtains and garlands hang at the corners of the sky. Dīpaṃkara, protector of others from sea monsters, is making the gesture of reassurance.

p.64: Add.1643, f.214v, *lp*. A stūpa in Tirabhukti (Tirhut, northern Bihār), with ten terraces and a cupola with a golden top and flowing banners. Two monks honour the stūpa.

p.66: Add.1643, f.169r, *rp*. A green Tārā in Tārāpura (Gujarat), making the gesture of giving and holding a lotus. She stands in a rock temple with masonry and is attended by a bluish-white bodhisattva, presumably a Tārā. Other cave temples contain a monk, a white god, a seated Buddha, and a wrathful attendant who wears a spotted dhoti and holds a club and noose. To the left, Kālādevī rides her mule.

p.69: Add.1643, f.147r, *lp*. A two-storey temple containing an Amitābha Buddha making the gesture of meditation and a white Avalokiteśvara making the gesture of giving and holding a lotus. In the left column is a yellow bodhisattva with a golden sceptre, probably Mañjuśrī, a green Tārā holding a lotus, and a female bodhisattva holding a club. The right column has a green bodhisattva holding a golden sceptre, probably Samantabhadra, a yellow Bhṛkuṭī Tārā with four arms, and a wrathful red Mārīcī making the gesture of remembering the Buddha.

p.70: Add.1643, f.133r, *rp*. A white Avalokiteśvara in a temple between trees in Daṇḍabhukti (West Bengal), making the gesture of giving. He holds a flask, a rosary and a lotus.

p.73: Add.1643, f.200v, *rp*. A wrathful red Mārīcī in Uḍḍiyāna (the Swat valley, northern Pakistan), with three faces, each with three eyes. She is swinging her eleven arms in a halo of flames. She holds a club, an elephant goad, a thunderbolt, an arrow, a sword, a red Aśoka flower (Saraca indica), a bow, a thread, Brahmā's severed head and a noose. She is making a threatening gesture (tarjanī mudrā).

p.74: Add.1643, f.220v, *rp*. A green Tārā in Rāḍha (West Bengal), lying on a bed beneath a tree and making a gesture of honouring. Behind the bed are three female attendants.

p.77: Add.1643, f.44r, *lp*. The historical Buddha making the gesture of teaching, seated on a lotus throne decorated with lions. Four elephants are honouring him, surrounded by trees. The image is from Kalaṣavarapura.

p.79: Add.1643, f.59v, *rp detail*. A green Tārā in an elaborate temple in Vārendrā (northwesten Bangladesh). She is making the gesture of giving and holding a lotus.

p.80: Add.1643, f.193r, *lp*. A white Avalokiteśvara on Jaya Mountain in Samataṭa (eastern Bangladesh), making the gesture of giving and holding a lotus. Beneath trees, a green Tārā is making the gesture of reassurance and a red Mārīcī is making the gesture of remembering the Buddha.

p.83: Add.1643, f.2v. The Buddha of the past, Dīpaṃkara (cf. p.63) in Java, making the gesture of reassurance. He is standing in a temple between trees with two bodhisattva attendants, a yellow Mañjuśrī and a white Avalokiteśvara, both making the gesture of explanation and holding a lotus.

p.86: Add.1643, f.20v, rp. The historical Buddha seated European style, teaching in a temple in Puṇḍavardhana (northern Bangladesh). Outside, two attendants, a white Avalokiteśvara and a green Vajrapāṇi, are seated on lotus thrones with stems, both holding a lotus.

p.88: Add.1464, f.2r, rp. A yellow Mañjughoṣa making the gesture of teaching, seated on a blue lion. He has a very indistinct blue lotus entwined around his arm. There are two attendants, probably a yellow Prince Sudhana and a blue Yamāri. His mandorla (almond-shaped halo) is similar to that of the Buddha in the centre panel of this folio (p.59), even in faded details like the cushion hatching. The left panel of this folio (p.99) also depicts a mandorla, though less clearly.

p.90: Add.1643, f.133r, lp detail. A white Avalokiteśvara sitting on a lotus in an ornate temple at Rādhya (northern Bihār), making the gesture of giving and holding a lotus. A dark banner snakes behind him.

p.93: Add.1643, f.80v, lp. A green Tārā in Candradvīpa (southern Bangladesh), making the gesture of giving and holding a lotus. In separate compartments, eight small Tārās hold lotuses.

p.95: Add.1464, f.226v, lp. A six-armed white Avalokiteśvara making the gestures of giving and explanation with two right hands. The other hands are not clearly distinguishable. He has one yellow attendant, maybe Prince Sudhana, and one red attendant who seems to be offering a pink lotus.

p.96: Add.1643, f.123v, lp. A very ornate golden stūpa with a parasol, against the night sky. The stūpa is encircled by a balustrade with a door on the left and enclosed in square walls at Puruṣapura, the capital of Gāndhāra (Peshawar, northern Pakistan). Originally a royal funeral mound, the stūpa became the primary Buddhist monument, a symbol of the Buddha.

p.99: Add.1464, f.2r, lp. A white Avalokiteśvara making the gesture of giving and wearing a loose meditation cord (cf. p.21). There is an uncoloured lotus to his left. One of his attendants seems to be a yellow Prince Sudhana making a gesture of honouring, holding a book to his chest, and wearing a five leafed crown. The other might be a red Abhimukha. He has long hair swept back from his face and is holding a staff.

p.100: Add.1643, f.202v, rp. A yellow Mañjughoṣa in China, making the gesture of teaching. He is seated on a blue lion and a lotus is entwined around his arm. He has two bodhisattva attendants, probably a yellow Prince Sudhana and a blue Yamāri (though looking similar to an Ekajaṭā, cf. p.88). They are in a cave temple in wooded mountains.

p.103: Add.1464, f.128r, cp. The Buddha making the gesture of teaching in the Jetavana grove at Śrāvasti, the capital of Kośala (southern Nepal), where he multiplied his form on countless lotus thrones. On either side of the Buddha his form is repeated, looking to the left and right (cf. p.13).

back endpapers: Add.1464, f.227r, rp. A yellow Tārā making the gesture of giving. Her left hand is possibly on her hip, holding a lotus. A green attendant is on the left. Nothing is clear due to the condition of the illustration.

Index to Characters and Places in the Illustrations

Glossary

abhaya mudrā the gesture of reassurance – usually right hand held palm outwards at chest level, fingers stretched.

adverse influences āsrava, 'outflows', the ties such as passion, desire for existence, wrong views and ignorance which bind a person to rebirth.

Ajita 'invincible', an epithet of Maitreya.

all-embracing knowledge sarvajñajñāna, often applied to the knowledge of a Buddha.

Amitābha 'immeasurable light', the Buddha of the western paradise (Sukhāvatī).

Ānanda the Buddha's cousin, personal attendant and one of his foremost disciples.

arhat 'worthy', someone who has gained insight into the true nature of things, exempt from further rebirths, but unable to teach others.

Aśoka Mauryan emperor of the 3rd century BCE.

Aṣṭasāhasrikāprajñāpāramitā *The Perfection of Wisdom in 8,000 Lines.*

Avalokiteśvara 'looks in every direction', a well-known bodhisattva who is the embodiment of compassion.

bases of sense perception āyatana: sight, hearing, smell, taste, touch and mind, and their respective objects.

Bhṛkuṭī Tārā Tārā 'with perfectly arched eyebrows'.

bhūmisparśa mudrā the earth witness gesture, made by the Buddha on the verge of enlightenment as the armies of Māra attacked him. He sits cross-legged, left hand palm upwards on his lap, third finger of his right hand touching the earth.

bodhisattva 'enlightenment being', a person who wishes to win full enlightenment and to help all beings do the same.

Brahmā the god Brahmā, seen in the past as the supreme being, the creator, yet still respected in Buddhism.

Buddha Enlightened One.

buddhasmaraṇa mudrā the gesture of remembering the Buddha – right hand held above the shoulder, palm outwards, fingers stretched or slightly bent.

components of personal existence skandha: form, feeling, perception, mental activities and consciousness.

contemplation dhyāna, one of the perfections.

dependent origination pratītyasamutpāda, a cycle of twelve specific conditions each dependent on the next, which expresses a Buddha's insight into saṃsāra.

dharmacakra mudrā the gesture of teaching – two hands, both with thumb and index finger touching, are held together, right palm outwards and left palm inwards.

dharmakāya the body of the teachings, the spiritual and absolute body of a Buddha symbolized by the stūpa.

dhyāna mudrā the gesture of meditation or contemplation – two hands joined palm upwards, with fingers stretched.

Dīpaṃkara a Buddha of the past.

Ekajaṭā or Ekajaṭī, 'one bun of hair', a blue Tārā also known as Ugratārā.

elements dhātu, things which make up the material world such as earth, water, fire and air.

giving dāna, one of the perfections.

Golden Flower Suvarṇapuṣpa, the goddess of the Ganges and a future Buddha.

Hayagrīva a god and a wrathful manifestation of Avalokiteśvara, usually wearing a horse's head.

India Jambudvīpa, the Land of the Rose-Apple Tree, is here translated very loosely as India. It is really the central - division of the world, in Buddhist cosmology one of the seven regions surrounding Mount Meru.

Indra chief of the gods, often called Śakra, and addressed as Kauśika.

irreversible avinirvarttanīya, incapable of turning back.

Jambhala god of wealth and consort of Vasudhāra, usually seen with his mongoose.

jñāna mudrā the gesture of knowledge – usually the left hand held palm inwards, with thumb and index finger touching.

Kālādevī the goddess Śrīdevī, often riding a mule.

karma action.

Kauśika an epithet of Indra.

Maitrāyaṇī Pūrṇa's mother.

Maitreya predicted to be the next Buddha and sometimes called Ajita.

makara a fish with an elephant's trunk.

mandorla or vesica, an almond-shaped body halo indicating a sacred figure.

Mañjughoṣa a form of Mañjuśrī.

Mañjuśrī a bodhisattva, who is forever young (kumārābhuta). Legend associates him with China.

Māra the Evil One, personification of all evils and passions.

Mārīcī 'beam of light', a goddess associated with dawn rituals and known for paralysing, bewildering and killing wicked beings.

Maudgalyāyana one of the Buddha's disciples, known for his supernatural powers and often paired with Śāriputra.

Māyā mother of the historical Buddha.

morality śīla, one of the perfections.

mudrā gesture of the hands and fingers to which a mystical significance is attached.

Nālāgiri the mad elephant who was calmed by the Buddha at Rājagrha.

namaskāra mudrā the gesture of honouring – two hands held palm to palm.

nirvāṇa liberation from the cycle of rebirth, transcending existence, being enlightened.

non-returner anāgamin, someone 'returning no more' to this world, who attains enlightenment in one of the heavens.

novice srotāpanna, someone 'entered into the stream', detached from mundane existence.

once-returner sakṛdāgamin, someone returning one final time to this world.

parinirvāṇa final, complete nirvāṇa at the time of death, extinction of the self.

patience kṣanti, one of the perfections.

perfections pāramitā. A bodhisattva masters giving, morality, patience, vigour, contemplation and wisdom.

Prajñāpāramitā *The Perfection of Wisdom*, also personified in the illustrations.

pratyekabuddha 'oneself-enlightened', a solitary enlightened being unable to teach others, symbolized by the rhinoceros.

predicted bodhisattva a bodhisattva whose enlightenment has been foretold by a Buddha.

Pūrṇa one of the Buddha's disciples and Maitrāyaṇī's son. He understands things well and exhibits great patience.

Rāhu a demon whose head was cut off for drinking the nectar of immortality.

realm of desire kāmādhātu, worlds where the inhabitants suffer from sensual desire, including this world.

realm of form rūpādhātu, worlds where the inhabitants have form, but do not suffer from sensual desire, including the heavens.

rūpakāya the physical body of a Buddha, the body of appearance symbolized by the sacred relics of a Buddha.

roots of virtue kuśalamūla, in particular avoidance of greed (alobha), malice (adoṣa), delusions (amoha). The roots of virtue provide the stock of merit which aids in progress towards enlightenment.

Śakra Indra.

Samantabhadra 'wholly auspicious', a bodhisattva.

saṃsāra the continual process of passing through a succession of states of existence.

Śāriputra one of the Buddha's foremost disciples, with less understanding than Subhūti and Pūrṇa. He is often paired with Maudgalyāyana.

skill in means upaya-kauśalya, adapting to circumstances.

stellar aeon tārakopama kalpa, a future era.

stūpa the quintessential Buddhist monument, containing relics or simply commemorating an event. Originally a funeral mound, usually of kings, it became the symbol of the Buddha, especially of his final entry into nirvāṇa.

Subhūti one of the Buddha's foremost disciples and one of the Elders (sthavira), he understands very well.

Sudhana Sudhanakumāra, the young prince who practises the perfection of vigour, learning from every situation.

Sugata 'well-gone', an epithet of a Buddha.

sūtra 'thread', dialogues, especially the texts which provide the primary source for a Buddha's teachings.

Tārā 'carrying across', a female bodhisattva associated with Avalokiteśvara.

tarjanī mudrā a threatening gesture – hand held in a fist with raised index finger.

Tathāgata 'thus-gone' or 'thus-come', an epithet of a Buddha, who has come as the other Buddhas have come.

Ugratārā a blue Tārā, a form of Ekajaṭā.

Vajrapāṇī 'wielding a thunderbolt', a bodhisattva.

varada mudrā the gesture of giving – usually the right arm is stretched out, palm upwards, fingers extended.

Vasudhārā goddess of wealth, consort of Jambhala.

vigour vīrya, one of the perfections.

vitarka mudrā the gesture of explanation – usually the right hand is raised palm outwards, with thumb and index finger touching and the other fingers extended.

Vulture Peak Gṛdhrakūṭa, a mountain site where the Buddha taught, not far from Rājagrha in Bihār.

wheel of the law dharmacakra, the wheel of the teaching – turning it is the symbol of teaching others.

wisdom or insight, prajñā, one of the perfections.

yakṣa mythical demons, often referred to as tree spirits or fairies. Some have accepted the teachings of the Buddha.

Yamāri a form of Yamāntaka, a god who is the enemy of Yama, lord of death.

Bibliography

Beautrix, Pierre; *Bibliographie de la littérature prajñāpāramitā*, Bruxelles: Institut belge des hautes études bouddhiques, 1971, (Publications de l'Institut belge des hautes études bouddhiques. Série Bibliographies; 3).

Conze, Edward; *Abhisamayālaṅkāra [of Maitreyanātha]*, Rome: Is. M.E.O., 1954, (Serie orientale Roma; vol. 6).

—; *The perfection of wisdom in eight thousand lines and its verse summary*, Bolinas: Four Seasons Foundation, 1973, (Wheel series; 1). A revised edition of his *Astasahasrika prajnaparamita [the perfection of wisdom in eight thousand slokas]*, Calcutta: Asiatic Society, 1958, (Bibliotheca Indica; issue number 1578, work number 284). This was reprinted in 1970 (Bibliotheca Indica; issue number 1592, work number 284). The 1973 edition has also been reprinted, Delhi: Satguru, 1994, (Bibliotheca Indo-Buddhica; 132).

—; *The prajñāpāramitā literature*, 's-Gravenhage: Mouton, 1960, (Indo-Iranian monographs; 6). Revised edition, Tokyo: Reiyuki, 1978, (Bibliographia philologica Buddhica. Series maior; 1).

Foucher, Alfred; *Étude sur l'iconographie bouddhique de l'Inde d'après des documents nouveaux*, 2 vols, Paris: A. Leroux, 1900-1905, (Bibliothèque de l'École des hautes études. Sciences religieuses; 13).

Losty, Jeremiah P.; *The art of the book in India*, London: British Library, 1982.

Mitra, Rājendrāla; *Ashtasāhasrikā: a collection of discourses on the metaphysics of the Mahāyāna school of the Buddhists*, Calcutta, 1887-1888, (Bibliotheca Indica. New series; 603, 620, 629, 645, 671, 690).

Obermiller, Eugene; *The doctrine of prajñāpāramitā as exposed in the Abhisamayālaṅkāra*, Acta Orientalia, vol. XI, pp. 1-133, 334-358, Copenhagen: 1933.

—; *Prajna paramita-ratna-guna-samcaya-gatha*, Leningrad: Academy of Sciences of the USSR, 1937, (Bibliotheca Buddhica; 29). Reprinted with added indexes, 's-Gravenhage: Mouton, 1960, (Indo-Iranian reprints; 5).

Ogiwara, Unrai; *Abhisamayālaṃkār'alokā prajñāpāramitāvyākhyā (commentary on Aṣṭasāhasrikā-prajñāpāramitā) by Haridhadra together with the text commented on*, Tokyo: The Toyo Bunko, 1932-35, (Toyo Bunko publications. Series D; v. 2).

Pal, Pratapaditya; *The arts of Nepal*, Leiden: E. J. Brill, 1974-1978, (Handbuch der Orientalistik: 7. Abt., Kunst und Archäologie; 3. Bd.; Innerasien, 3. Abschnitt; Tibet, Nepal, Mongolei, 2. Lfg.).

Pal, Pratapaditya and Meech-Pekarik, Julia; *Buddhist book illuminations*, New York: Ravi Kumar, c.1988.

Saraswati, Sarasi Kumar; *Tantrayāna art: an album*, Calcutta: The Asiatic Society, 1977.

Snellgrove, David L., *The image of the Buddha*, London: Serindia 1978.

Author Acknowledgments

There are many people I would like to thank. His Holiness the Dalai Lama, for taking an interest in this book and for providing its foreword. Philip Denwood, knowledgeable about Buddhist architecture, who was also my first teacher of Tibetan. Professor Emeritus David Snellgrove, who was my main teacher in London, while he was working on his *The Image of the Buddha*. Friedhelm Hardy, who was my first serious teacher of Sanskrit. Helmut Neumann, who has read the proofs and commented on many aspects of the book. Various other readers, some with particular expertise, some as general readers, who have read parts of this work at various stages and helped to form it into its final shape. Caroline Davidson, who has taken a keen interest and guided me through the world of publishing. At Frances Lincoln, Cathy Fischgrund, the commissioning editor who first sparked this project and who has been thoroughly committed to it at every stage. Fiona Robertson, who has been an assistant editor caring for detail well beyond my own eye and putting much of her own understanding into the book. Trish Going's design work has resulted in the book you have before you – which speaks for itself. And most importantly, Shirley Jamieson, who has helped in countless significant ways.

2001